2,50

How to Study

How to Study

by

LAWRENCE S. FINKEL

and

RUTH KRAWITZ

Illustrations by

DUANE UNKEFER

1964

Oceana Publications, Inc.

Dobbs Ferry, New York

Table of Contents

How to Study

THE TIME HAS COME

If you are a fifth or sixth grader, you have already spent about 9,500 hours of your life in school, sitting across from teachers and teachers and more teachers. This means you are a "pupil." Is this enough? Are you just a "pupil," or can you call yourself a "student?" There is a difference. The student does more than occupy space in the classroom. He uses what he is taught. He has learned how to think. He has learned how to study.

"TEST YOURSELF—Are you "pupil" or "student"?

Do you take an active part in your classwork?
Do you ask for help when you have a problem?
Do you make homework a help in learning?
Do you plan your work?
Do you understand how to use the materials for your work?
Do you use more than one source to find information?
Do you put knowledge to work?

WHAT IS STUDYING?

Studying is an art. It is important to know *how* in order to get the most out of it. You may have good intentions, you may be trying very hard, yet, you may not be getting good results. You may even be like Larry—

Larry decides to do his studying after dinner. He takes out his books, places them on the table next to the most comfortable chair in the living room, arms himself with fruit and candy, in case he should feel hungry, then settles into the chair, ready to work. He starts by searching for the scrap of paper on which his homework assignment was written. He finds that his pencils need sharpening. "Stick-them-up," cries a voice on the television, and he runs off to watch. "Back to your homework," says Mother. Slowly he returns to his books. Next, he looks for the arithmetic books which he left in the classroom. He goes back to the comfortable chair to daydream about sinking the winning basket in Saturday's game. When Mother calls, "Bedtime," Larry realizes that in two hours he has accom-

146970

plished nothing. "Anyway," he says to himself, "I'll do the assignment in the morning," although he knows that usually he just manages to get to school on time.

Is this the way you study? If so, it's time to improve your study habits, or form new ones. Good study habits are as easy to follow as bad ones. The more efficiently you study, the better grades you will earn, and the more free-time you will have to enjoy.

LEARNING BY LISTENING

Studying begins at school. Your teacher *tells* you what to study. Your first job is to pay attention in class. Books are very important, but they cannot take the place of your teacher. You can learn by listening to her. Guess how many hours you spend in school listening. Almost fifteen hours every week are spent listening, for many different reasons.

One way to improve your listening is by understanding the reason for it. Are you enjoying a story the teacher is telling? Are you following directions to perform some task? Are you trying to understand an assignment? Is answering questions your purpose? Listening with a purpose makes you an active listener. Don't be a half-listener. Don't tune the teacher in and out, like a radio. Follow carefully what is being said. Be a responsible listener.

THE NOTEBOOK HABIT

Another responsibility you have is to copy your homework assignment correctly. Develop the notebook habit and use it properly. Keep a small notebook especially for homework assignments. Copy directions carefully. Include the date the assignment is due. Don't hesitate to ask the teacher questions when you don't understand exactly what you are to do at home.

15

TIME TO STUDY

Now you know *what* to study. Your teacher may suggest *how much time* to spend each day. "Fitting it in" is up to you. Begin by preparing a time schedule for yourself. First, list your responsibilities, such as: music lessons, dancing lessons, shopping, household chores, Boy Scout meetings, Girl Scout meetings, etc. This will give you an idea of how many hours you have in your day for the business of study. Your time schedule might look something like this:

9 - 3	School
3 - 4	Play
4 - 5	Piano Lessons
5 - 6	Dinner
6 - 7	Household chores
7 - 8	
8 - 9	
9	Bedtime

With this schedule, the hours between 7 and 9, after dinner and before bedtime, are available for homework assignments. Most children prefer this time. If, however, you have a favorite television program which you would like to watch between 8 and 9, then you might study between seven and eight. Choose, from the unclaimed hours in your day, as much time as you need to complete the job or learn the lesson. Whatever study time you choose—give yourself enough of it. Pick an early hour, so that you are still wide awake. You'll get the best results if you make studying a routine like eating or sleeping. Try to do your work about the same time each day. Time is the first tool of study—make wise use of it.

BUDGET WISELY

Time can be friend or foe. Some children have too much of it, others never seem to have enough. Just as your mother must plan her time to keep the household running smoothly, so must you budget your study time. The amount of time you spend studying at home depends on two things:

— how much homework your teacher has given you and

— how well you are doing in your school work.

If you are an elementary school boy or girl, you should try to study an hour each evening, with the exception of Friday or Saturday and Sunday which may be left free for fun. In junior high school, that time is usually expanded to an hour and a half on each study night. This way, you will be prepared for each school day, and ready to enjoy your free nights.

A PLACE TO STUDY

You know *what*. You know *when*. The next step is *where*. Think again about our friend, Larry . . . and that easy chair in the living room. Is it a good place to study? Hardly! Your mother and father, delighted with your new willingness, will help you find a good study corner. No matter where you live, small apartment or house, such a place can be arranged. It may be your own room, or a corner of the kitchen or living room.

You need a table or desk, a comfortable straight chair (not one you can snooze in), a good light and a quiet place. Have only the things you will use in front of you—books, paper, pencils, pen, eraser, ruler. Put away anything that might distract you—clocks, pictures, playthings. Do you have two heads? Our friend, Larry, must. How else can he study and listen to the phonograph or the television at the same time! If *you* try to do this, your studying will suffer, and you will be spending more time on it than is necessary.

Are you ready to plunge in now? Let's make sure. Use this check list to see how well prepared you are.

WHAT IS YOUR "GRQ" (GETTING READY QUOTIENT)?

Do you . . .   Yes   No

1. Ask questions in class when you are not sure of something?

2. Write your assignment in a notebook?

3. Try to find something interesting in each subject?

4. Usually study in the same place each day?

5. Keep your desk or table clear of distractions?

6. Have enough light so that you can read without eyestrain?

7. Keep radio and TV turned off?

8. Discourage interruptions, such as family conversations and telephone calls?

9. Study in a quite place?

10. Have the necessary materials on hand?

11. Finish one assignment before leaving it?

12. Do written assignments on time or before they are due?

13. Make and follow a time schedule?

14. Budget your study time?

                                            Score

21

HOW TO REMEMBER

If you cannot remember what you have studied, you haven't really learned it. Two of the ways to memorize are, (1) automatically, and (2) with reasoning or understanding. The first way, you say something over and over again until you can remember it. Then you can recite word-for-word what you studied. Does this mean that you understand it? Of course not. This simply means that you can spout like a parrot. There are times when it is neces-

sary and important to learn this way. In arithmetic, for example, you must memorize tables so that you can use them correctly and instantly. In social studies you memorize many dates and events. In language arts there are poems to be memorized, perhaps a part in the school play, and of course, spelling words.

However, you must be able to tell what you have learned in your own words, in order to prove you understand it. To memorize with reasoning you think about what you are learning and understand it thoroughly. Later, you may not be able to repeat the material word-for-word. Instead, you will be able to talk or write about what you learned, intelligently, in your own words. You use this kind of memorizing in social studies, in story-discussions, in composition-writing. You can probably think of times when both kinds of memorization are used hand-in-hand. For example, you would use automatic memory to recall important facts in the life of Abraham Lincoln in order to discuss, with understanding, his contributions as a great president.

What you are studying, and *why* you are studying, will help you choose the Memory Method best for you. If you know the reason for memorizing something, you will learn it faster and remember it longer. To use either system you must test yourself again and again as you are learning, until saying or writing the material becomes routine. Then review what you have learned. In a few hours test yourself again. Repeat the test a few days later. Do you still need practice? Review your Memory Method.

The most important step in learning to remember is to see the whole picture clearly. Psychologists call this the "whole" method of learning. In both kinds, the automatic and the reasoning, it is better to learn using the "whole" method rather than the "part" method. So, if you are memorizing a song, it is best to do it as a whole from beginning to end. If you try learning one line thoroughly before going on to the next, you will spend a great deal more time on the first few lines than any others. Think about this! Isn't it so? You sing or recite the lines until you make a mistake. Then what do you do?Go right back to the beginning and try again! The poor lines in the middle or at the end are often sadly neglected in the practicing, and completely forgotten in the reciting. Don't play favorites! Give all parts of what you are studying an equal share of your attention.

HELPFUL HINTS

How many tips for remembering do you know? Recently, our friend, Larry, surprised everyone in class, especially the teacher, by volunteering to answer the question, "What are the names of the five Great Lakes?" Afterwards he boasted to his admiring classmates, "There was nothing to it! All I had to do was remember the word HOMES, and the names came easily." Larry used a catchword to help him remember. Each letter of the word HOMES stands for one of the Great Lakes. Some people use rhymes or formulas to help remember certain facts and figures. When you need to know the number of days in a particular month, don't you think of the ditty:

Thirty days hath September
April, June and November. . . .

Many people even make up "memory gimmicks" of their own. These tricks are sometimes called crutches because they help you get over a memory obstacle. Like all crutches, the sooner you can do without them, the better. You don't need crutches if your legs are mended. You won't need memory crutches when you've learned your facts and figures thoroughly. Use them only as long as you need them. Consistent practice and review will help you get rid of them.

Here are other hints to help you remember. Try fixing the facts by writing them down. This will leave your mind free to concentrate on the parts that are hardest.

Use this technique to practice the next time your teacher gives you a spelling assignment. You'll like the results!

1. Look at the word. Pronounce it. Think of the meaning. Spell it orally.

2. Write the word from memory. Compare it with the correct spelling.

If Correct

Write the word again from memory. Compare it with the sample.

If Not Correct

Look for the spot that was hard for you.
Plan how best to "fix" the spelling.
Write and compare the word until you have written it three or even more times without missing.

Look back. You were asked to write each word as well as say it aloud. Looking at the word helps. Looking at the word and saying it helps even more. Looking at the word, saying it aloud, and writing it down is best. This is "active" learning. You are learning by seeing, by hearing and by doing. You are using your senses to help you.

WHAT'S YOUR "MMQ" (MEMORY METHOD QUOTIENT)?

Do you . . .   Yes No
1. Understand why you need to know this material?
2. Put the things you are learning into your words?
3. Try to see the "whole" picture of what is to be learned?
4. Say it aloud?
5. Write it down?
6. Use "crutches" when you need them, and discard them when you don't?
7. Try to tie it up with what you already know?
8. Keep your mind on your studies?
9. Study when you are alert?

Score:

MAKING THE MOST OF READING

You probably think of studying as a homework assignment or a review before a test. Actually, it is any activity through which you get or give information and ideas. Studying may even be reading a textbook. Experts say that about 90 per cent of all your study activities, at school and at home, require reading. Reading and learning are so closely related that in order to learn well you must read well.

Much of your work, both in the classroom and at home, involves reading for facts. This is the kind of reading your mother does when she reads the morning paper, or a new recipe. Dad reads for facts when he studies directions for a do-it-yourself project, or price lists down at his office, or stock market figures. A large part of the reading in every person's day involves reading for facts.

The teacher may assign many different kinds of fact-reading jobs. She may ask you to read a certain number of pages to prepare for the next day's lesson. Often, there will be questions to answer as well. She may assign a topic for research, or you may want to learn more about a topic the class is discussing. In all these jobs you must read to get the information. Are you able to do these reading jobs well?

Do you know what to do when your teacher asks you to read certain pages and answer specific questions? Begin by writing down the questions. Turn to the pages you are to read. Refer to your questions and look for key words, the important words in the question. Underline these key words. Keeping them in mind, look quickly at your book. Are there paragraph headings in heavy print? Are any of your key words in the paragraph heading? How about pictures? Are there any that might help you find the answer to your questions? Glance at your maps, graphs and charts. They might contain the clues you need.

Having looked through the assignment you have found those paragraphs, pictures, maps and graphs which are important to you. Now go back to your questions and begin taking notes. Refer to the pictures, maps and graphs wherever necessary.

Some reading assignments will require only skimming. Skimming is reading quickly to find important facts or ideas.

When you skim, you:
1. Keep in mind what you are looking for.
2. Need to have questions in mind.
3. Read rapidly.
4. Keep going and do not look back.
5. Slide over unimportant words.
6. Do not try to remember or understand everything, but look for your answer.
7. Stop and read carefully the answer to your question.

People read at different speeds. Poor readers read everything at the same slow rate. Good readers have many reading rates. The kind of reading, and the speed with which you read, depend on what you are studying and why. You undoubtedly read your social studies text much more quickly than your science book. You read a story faster than a problem. You can save time by reading different kinds of material at different speeds. Regardless of your reading speed you can almost surely increase it.

This might help you.

If you read every text or article at the same speed, then you should try to . . . . . . fit your rate to the difficulty of the material. Read a text-book slowly, a story book rapidly.

If you read sentence by sentence, from beginning to end, then you should try to . . . . scan first, to get the main ideas. This helps you to read rapidly with more understanding.

If you read word by word, then you should try to . . . . . look for thoughts or phrases. You can learn to see a few words in the time it takes you to read one.

If you move your head as you read, then you should try to . . . . move your eyes instead. It is easier and not so tiring.

If you move your lips as you read, then you should . . . put your fingers on your lips and move your eyes only.

If you often reread, then you should . . . . read easier material and practice going right ahead. Then go on to harder things. Don't go back, keep reading ahead. You'll soon realize that you are getting the meaning the first time.

If you sometimes forget what you have just read, you should try to . . . . read with a definite idea in mind. Get the main idea; remember important facts; use what you have learned.

How to Take A Test

How to Take A Test

Test today! Got the shivers? Nervous? Worried? Sick to your stomach? You're not alone, friend. Students, everywhere, react just this way. Some become violently upset, others only mildly so. But the jitters are there. You might as well stop worrying. Like it or not, tests are definitely here to stay.

39

Tests are a help to your teacher. They give her a chance to know you better. They keep her up to date with your progress in class. They tell her what you have yet to learn. They help her to plan work for you. These are the ways tests help her. How about you?

Tests tell what you have done, and how much more you can do. If you have any unawakened interests, tests will tell. Where do you stand in spelling or arithmetic or science, compared with the other children in your class, or in your school? Tests will tell. What help, if any, do you need in your school work? Do you have any special abilities or talents in the fields of art or music or crafts? Tests will tell the story.

Everyone today is test-conscious, so don't blame tests only on school. Care to attend West Point? You must pass a test. Want a commission in the Armed Forces? You must pass a test. Thinking about a Civil Service job? You must pass a test. You will even have to pass a test to drive an automobile. In today's world of work, many better-paying jobs and promotions are determined by tests. So, stop your grumbling. Tests are not a trap. You can use them as a crystal ball to learn more about yourself.

40

DON'T BE AFRAID

Make every test a game. Fear is your opponent. It stands in the way of your winning the game. When you are afraid, you cannot think clearly. You make careless mistakes. You may fail to read questions correctly, or miss key words in questions, or read only parts of questions. Are you going to let fear defeat you? You don't have to! Practice the hints given in the first part of this book and you will have started to knock Mr. Fear out of the game. Your good study habits should prepare you well. They are an important step toward meeting the challenge and winning the game.

HOW TO REVIEW

Your teacher has announced a test. Do you know how to prepare for it? Do you know when to review and where to begin? The answer is *right away and every day.* Before you leave the class check your notebook and if you have missed any assignments catch up as quickly as possible. Ask questions if there is something you can't remember, so that you can review alone at home.

Half-hearted studying is not reviewing. The most important tip for reviewing is to concentrate on the subject before you. In addition, go over what you have studied or talked about in class. Skim your textbook and the notes that you have taken. You should glance over old tests and quizzes to make sure that you have corrected all the wrong answers, and know the right ones. Reviewing is bound to be less of a problem if you learned the material well at the beginning. Remember, reviewing is not the same as studying.

To get the best results from reviewing it should be as different from studying as you can make it. Make the facts you learned come alive. For example, plan a current newscast of history facts. Use all your senses for reviewing. Be as active a reviewer as you were a learner.

Be your own Question-and-Answer man. Make up questions and try to answer them. Use paper and pencil as much as you can. Underline! Outline! List points! Diagram! Draw a map! Do any or all of these things if they help you. As you come to the end of a section you are reviewing, stop, lean back, and think. Change a topic sentence to a question. Can you answer it? Keep alert for points that would make good test questions. Try to guess some of these questions. What items did the teacher stress in class? What does the textbook say is important?

REVIEWING TOGETHER

Do you work well, preparing for a test with your friends? Working with a friend, or a group of friends, is good if you remember to stick to the job at hand. It is amazing how many reviewers find it necessary to study the contents of the refrigerator, or the channels on the nearest television set. Neither do friends' telephone numbers need to be studied. Studying together, if you do not lose sight of your goal, *can be* worthwhile. It can be a

44

check to discover if anyone in the group has neglected something. Here are some rules to follow:

1. There should be no more than five children in the group.
2. Meetings should be short — in general, not longer than an hour.
3. There should be one meeting to plan the responsibilities of each member of the group.
4. Each member should bring to the next meeting an outline or summary of what he has prepared.
5. At the next few meetings, ask each other questions. Summarize important points for one another. Take an old idea and tell it as though the others had never heard it before.

After studying together a few times, you will know if group-reviewing is best for you. Try it! But keep in mind, it's review, not play, you are after.

PRE-TEST TACTICS

A sure-fire pre-test tactic, whether you review alone or with friends, is to concentrate hardest on what you do not know. For example, if you are reviewing for a spelling test, don't bother with those words that you already know. Spend your time practicing the words which you are not sure of and those you do not know. For other subjects, go over facts or items that seem to slip your mind easily, or that you had difficulty understanding at the beginning.

SCHEDULING TEST-STUDY TIME

By now, you should have made Time a friend. Draw up and stick to a test-study schedule, just as you did a Time Schedule for Study. If you are in an elementary

school taking a test, give yourself some time in your daily study schedule to prepare for it. If you are a Junior High School youngster, faced with many examinations, spend some time with each subject. Give your weakest subjects the most time. Study them first, while you are still wide awake. Make every effort to stick to your schedule. However, don't be a slave to the schedule — it's supposed to serve you. If you find that your original schedule is not the best arrangement, change it. Perhaps you need more time for some subjects than for others. Perhaps the hours that you planned to study are not convenient. There's that Boy Scout meeting that you have been looking forward to! Or that important telecast that the teacher suggested you watch! Don't worry. Change your schedule to meet your needs.

GETTING IN SHAPE

We have suggested that you treat each test as a game or contest. Train for the test as the athlete would train for a game or contest. Be prepared physically as well as mentally. Get plenty of sleep. To be wide-awake, you need to be well-rested. Not enough sleep means a tired body. A tired body means a tired mind. And who ever heard of writing a good examination with a tired mind! Eat the right foods. This is no time for ice cream with pickles. A stomach ache is sure to follow. These are not the foods your body needs to give you the energy for test-taking. Find time for fun and play. Remember that all work and no play can make you, and Larry, dull boys!

Just as a runner trains for his track meet by running every day for months, so you too must train over a long period of time by doing the things you will have to do on examination day. Try to study under the same conditions you will meet on that day. There is no substitute for this training period. You will never be prepared by leaving it for the last day or two before the contest. You will be calm, relaxed and sure of yourself if you study the material regularly, as we suggested. This is the right way to feel!

What happens to those children who always put off till tomorrow the studying they could have done today or yesterday, or the day before? Your friend, Larry, is one of those who always puts off his studying until the last minute. A typical Larry result . . . tired body . . . tired mind . . . tired grade! Larry's idea of studying is to cram. He confuses cramming with reviewing. He substitutes cramming for reviewing.

Teachers agree that cramming is a good way to guarantee poor test results. Can you imagine baseball players forgetting pre-season training? Would they leave the practicing until a few hours before game-time? What a loss that game would be. You cannot leave your studying until the evening before the test and hope to review everything you need to know. This is the night to spend reviewing briefly, going over some troublesome detail. And this shouldn't take too long. This is the night to relax, and get to bed early. Cramming exhausts you both physically and mentally. A tired mind and body are useless.

WHAT'S YOUR "P.Q." (PREPARATION QUOTIENT)?

You should now be ready to tackle that test. Are you? Find out by checking your "P.Q"

Do you . . .   Yes   No
  1. Keep up your daily work?
  2. Review your work regularly?
  3. Review your work actively?

4. Get help from your teacher when you are unsure of the material?
5. Concentrate on the things you do not know?
6. Draw up and try to stick to a test-study schedule?
7. Keep yourself in top physical health?
8. Consider the test a challenge and not a trap?
9. Review only briefly just before the examination?
10. Go to bed at your regular time the night before the test?

Score:

TYPES OF TESTS

Generally speaking, there are two kinds of tests. One is called the essay type, the other the objective type. The essay type is often called the "long-answer" test. The objective type is called the "short-answer" test. You will meet both, often, during your school career. The tests you will take will be one type or the other. Sometimes, however, a test will combine both types.

An essay test gives you a chance to write your ideas clearly, using your own words. You are expected to answer the question completely.

The objective test asks questions that call for answers you give by choosing (multiple-choice), checking (matching), filling in blanks (completion), or marking right or wrong (true-false).

51

The differences are easy to see. One has short answers. The other asks for long answers. Since objective tests call only for short answers, they usually have many more questions. One may have as many as 50 to 100 questions, while an essay test may have only two or three questions. A most important difference is that your teacher must mark your answer in the objective test either all right or all wrong, while in the essay test she may give you partial credit for an answer.

TACKLING THE ESSAY

If you were able to pass the "P.Q." with flying colors, then you should be able to face any essay test with confidence. This is why we have suggested that you review regularly. Each study period is a rehearsal. It is wise to keep in mind that unimportant details will not be asked for in an essay test. Only the important information that you covered in your schoolwork will be covered on the test. With this in mind, let's go on to the test itself.

You would agree that it's not a good idea to dive into a pool of water without knowing the depth of the water. It's just as foolish to jump into the writing of a test-answer before giving it some thought and preparing an outline. Jot down your ideas. Organize them in outline form with a major idea, and supporting ideas. Rearrange them if necessary. Then use this outline to write your answer. Check your outline, make sure you followed the teacher's orders. Does she want you to *describe, explain, compare,* or *list?* Don't waste time doing more than is asked for. This will not improve your grade. Do exactly what you have been asked to do.

A bluffer is easy to spot! Don't be one! Be direct and to the point. Write your answer as briefly as possible, but without leaving anything out.

Write your answers legibly. After all your preparation, surely you want the teacher to be able to read the test. If she cannot read your writing, she cannot give you credit for the answer. So . . . . . don't be sloppy. *Dot your i's, cross your t's and mind your p's and q's.*

Slang is out! Using a slang word or expression in your test answer is showing poor taste. Take extra care with your spelling, punctuation and capitalization. Your teacher may deduct points for incorrect grammar and mispelled words.

Above all, make sure that you understand and follow the directions. This is very important. If you aren't careful, all too late, you may find yourself doing something you were not asked to do. Think of all the precious time you wasted!

Your next step is to read all the questions, not just the first one. This will give you a clear picture of what the test is about. Find the questions that have things in common. Notice whether you are expected to answer all parts of all questions. Some tests say, "Answer three of the following five questions" . . . or something like that. Make a mental note of whether some questions count more than others. Then budget your time. As you read the test, estimate how much time you think you will need for each question. Allow additional minutes for reading the entire test, and for a review when you are finished. If you have an hour to answer five questions, allow no more than 10 minutes for each. You will need the extra 10 minutes for your preparation and review. However, the more difficult a question is, or the more points it gives you, the more time you should allow for working on it.

Answer the easy questions first. These will, of course, be the ones you're sure you know the answers to. If you read a question and are stumped—leave it for a while. Plan to come back to it later. At least you'll be making certain that you get credit for the things you do know. It's even possible, that while you are answering the questions you're sure of, some idea will come to you about the *hard* ones. Your mind is a complicated thing. It can unconsciously be thinking about the difficult items while you are answering the easy ones. It may be that some idea in an answer you are writing will give you the hint you need for a difficult question. Just like that, the question may no longer be a problem!

At the end of the exam, you should have some time left. Reread your paper. Be sure that you answered all parts of all questions. Correct your paper. Does it say what you wanted to say? Reread your paper again. Have you used proper English to say what you wanted to say? Are words spelled correctly? Do all sentences begin with a capital letter and end with the correct punctuation mark?

OBJECTIVE TESTS

Of the two types of tests, the objective, or short-answer, seems to be the more popular. Children call it "the kind where you're asked to make tiny pencil marks in the right places." Let's look at some of these objective tests

MULTIPLE CHOICE

A favorite type of question is multiple-choice. In a multiple-choice test, you are given part of a sentence, and several choices with which to complete it. One of the choices is correct; the others are incorrect. For example:
Directions:

> Circle the letter indicating the correct number in the sentence below.

The Sahara is (a) the only hot desert in the world, (b) the largest desert in the world, (c) a large desert in the western part of our country, (d) a high mountain range.

To answer this question correctly you should circle the letter (b).

COMPLETION

Completion tests are very much like multiple-choice. However, instead of selecting the best answer from a group of answers, you must supply the answer yourself, in the blank provided. This completion question tests your ability to remember specific facts, such as a name or date. For example:

Directions: Fill in the blank.

The first successful steam engine was invented by ——————————. To answer this question correctly you should write in the name James Watts.

TRUE-FALSE

In a true-false test, you are given a statement, and are asked to tell whether it is correct or incorrect. In this kind of test, you may come across such words as *always, never, all,* or *none.* A question that has such words in it should make you suspicious. It is almost always false. If the words *should* or *must* are used, the answer is usually false. The words *might* or *may* in the question mean it is usually true.

Students often ask the question, "Is it wise to guess, or should I skip the question if I don't know the answer?" Usually, it is better to guess. On most of the questions, you'll probably have some inkling of an idea. That mind of yours may work subconsciously again, sending you clues here and there.

A true-false test item might look like this:

Directions: Place T in space after question if true; F if false.

————The new world had been discovered before Columbus made his voyage.

You would answer this question correctly by putting a "T" in the blank.

MATCHING

A matching-type test is a favorite among teachers. It usually consists of two lists—an item in one list is to be matched with an item in the other. Most matching tests ask you to link together names of places and their location, authors and their books, events and dates, places and products, or words and their meanings. A good way to help you answer this kind of question, is to draw a light pencil line from the item in one column to its matching item in the other column. This shows you quickly how many you are sure of. Another way is to cross off each item as you list each letter so you can easily see how many you have left to use. This is called the "process of elimination". It may help you through the whole question, even if you know only some of the answers. Try this one:

Directions: Before each item in List 1, write the letter from List 2 which gives its meaning. List 2 has one extra meaning See how well you can do using the "process of elimination."

List 1 — Words	List 2 — Meanings
———1. mile	a. 60 seconds
———2. minute	b. less time than one second
———3. 30 seconds	c. 2000 feet
———4. 4/5 of a second	d. one-half minute
———5. an inch and a half	e. 5280 feet
	f. more than one inch and less than two inches

Following instructions is an absolute must when you are taking an objective test. Misreading a single word, or checking or underlining a different answer from the one you really intended, can make your errors mount. Use these tips for objective-test-taking.

TIPS FOR TEST-TAKING

Work at a rate comfortable for you. Keep calm. Don't be stampeded into a pace that will panic you. When you come to a question that stumps you—skip it. You cannot

59

afford to give any one question more than its share of time. You can go back to troublesome questions when you are all finished. Then complete them as best you can. Reread them. There may have been a clue in some of the later questions you answered which can help you with those you had to skip at the beginning. Remember! Your first answer is usually the correct one. Think twice before you change it. Don't make any changes without fairly good reasons.

WHAT'S YOUR "TTQ" (TEST-TAKING QUOTIENT)?

Have you . . .   Yes   No
1. Read your instructions carefully?
2. Looked over the entire test before beginning?
3. Answered the easier questions first?
4. Given more time to those questions that gave more credit?
5. Looked for key words?
6. Checked to see that you included all the material that you intended?
7. Reread your paper for careless mistakes or omissions?
8. Written legibly?

Score:

A FINAL WORD ON TESTS

When your test paper is returned to you, it can be very helpful. Your teacher has probably put a grade on your paper. She will undoubtedly have indicated which

questions you answered correctly, and which ones you answered incorrectly. Your job is to find out *why* you made the mistakes. For example, you may find that although you understood your work, you couldn't put your ideas into words. You may have read the questions incorrectly. You may simply not have known the answers. You may have prepared the wrong topics. Whatever mistakes you made, try to avoid them in the future. Look up the correct answers to every question you missed. Study them carefully. Ask your teacher about anything you still do not understand. In the same way, look carefully at those parts of the test on which you did best. What was there about the answers that made them outstanding? This kind of self-checking will help you learn more about a subject. It will certainly help you with your next test.

A FINAL WORD OF CAUTION

You met our friend, Larry. Through him, you have seen that there is a right and a wrong way to study. Don't be like Larry. There is no short cut to studying. There is no easy way to success with your schoolwork.

Just as a workman needs his tools to complete his task, so you need your tools to complete yours. Just as an athlete must train for his contest, so you must train for yours.

Your job at this time in your life is attending school. A major challenge is taking tests. Be a true craftsman. Be a good athlete. Take the tools we have given you and use them well.

Needless to say, you will not receive any salary for doing your job. You will, however, receive values that money cannot buy—satisfaction in a job well done, and the reward of continuing success in high school and the privilege of going to college.

A WORD TO THE WISE

There is a big difference between a pupil and student. It is not a matter of luck or looks. It is the ability to know HOW TO STUDY.